# Yorkshire Dales
## Souvenir Guide

compiled by Andrew Gallon

**Dalesman**
*visitor guides*

**First published in 2012 by Dalesman**
**an imprint of Country Publications Ltd**
The Water Mill, Broughton Hall
Skipton
North Yorkshire
BD23 3AG

www.dalesman.co.uk

© Dalesman 2012
Photographs © individual photographers as listed on page 64

Cover: Wildflower meadow near Muker

ISBN 978-1-85568-301-3

Printed in China by 1010 Printing

Designed by Black Dog Industries

Ask a hundred visitors what they love most about the Yorkshire Dales and the chances are you'll get a hundred different answers. The allure of the Dales is varied, complex and above all enduring. It might be the glorious scenery that sets the pulse racing, perhaps the attractive towns and villages or breathtaking structures, the dramatically unpredictable weather, the majestic rivers and waterfalls, or maybe even the friendly folk who are lucky enough to live, work and play in such an inspiring corner of the world.

This pictorial guide, featuring images from Britain's leading photographers, contains many of the elements which, taken together, ensure the endlessly fascinating Dales remain a supremely popular tourist destination. In the pages that follow, roam with us across the length and breadth of this magnificent landscape, and enjoy the atmospheric Dales throughout every season and in all their moods.

It's quite a journey!

# Made a Vale

**Main:** An exquisite panorama from a perch above the linear Wensleydale village of Carperby, with the 1,727-foot (526m) summit of Penhill a striking backdrop along the valley's southern flank.

**Inset:** A farmer marshals his sheep on the verdant floor of Dentdale, home to the River Dee.

**Right:** A spectacular view from the upper reaches of Deepdale, looking down this short tributary valley towards neighbouring Dentdale.

# Made a Vale

**Left:** An inviting gap stile punctures a beautifully crafted drystone wall in Bishopdale, a peaceful valley which provides a link between Wensleydale and Wharfedale.

**Middle:** A vertical slice of lovely Coverdale, looking south over the rooftops of Horsehouse, the valley's prettiest village.

**Right:** Viewed from Twisleton Scars, Ingleborough, at 2,372 feet (723m) the second highest of Yorkshire's famous Three Peaks, keeps watch over a distinctly wintry Chapel-le-Dale scene.

# Made a Vale

**Right:** Rather more than a touch of frost along the banks of the 127-mile (204km) Leeds-Liverpool Canal as it passes through Farnhill in Airedale.

**Left:** Garsdale, broad and green, seen from the lower slopes of Winder, one of the shapely Howgill Fells rising behind Sedbergh.

# Stairways to Heaven

**Left:** Simon's Seat, a notable Wharfedale peak rising to 1,591 feet (485m), glowers over the village of Appletreewick on a chilly day.

**Top right:** Kisdon, a shapely hill in upper Swaledale with a high point of 1,636 feet (499m), seen from the green lane which contours along the valley's southern flank and links Muker with Thwaite.

**Bottom right:** A rocky cairn marking High Seat's summit is the perfect vantage point from which to admire Wild Boar Fell, Mallerstang Dale's most distinctive hill. It is named after the wild boars which once roamed here.

**Below:** The war memorial crowning the 1,650-foot (503m) summit of Cracoe Fell. A prominent obelisk, it is a familiar sight to motorists using the road between Skipton and Threshfield.

# Going with the Flow

**Far right:** The multiple tiers of Scaleber Force, formed by Scaleber Beck tumbling over a series of rocky ledges in the hills above Settle.

**Right:** Hellgill Force dramatically lit on a stormy day. This 25-foot (8m) waterfall, close to the Yorkshire-Cumbria border near the head of Mallerstang Dale and a two-minute walk from the B6259, is on Hell Gill Beck, which soon becomes the infant River Eden.

**Left:** Stainforth Force, a multi-tiered waterfall on the Ribble, is a great spot to watch salmon leaping in October and November. Here, an adult salmon negotiates this major obstacle as it heads upstream to spawn.

# Going with the Flow

**Left:** The constricted environs of Mill Gill Force, one of several stunning Wensleydale waterfalls in the vicinity of Askrigg.

**Middle:** Thornton Force, the pick of numerous breathtaking cascades on the Ingleton Waterfalls Trail. Here, the Twiss, which begins its life as Kingsdale Beck, drops suddenly and dramatically into a wooded gorge.

**Right:** Hardraw Force, at 100 feet (30m) the longest single-drop waterfall in England. In the foreground, Hardraw Beck races off towards the Green Dragon Inn, where admission to this rocky amphitheatre can be obtained.

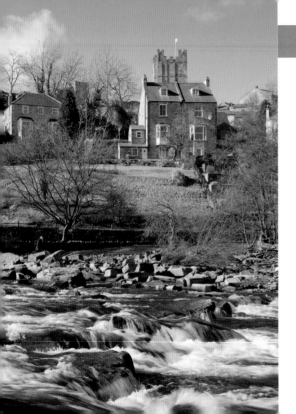

# Mystic Rivers

**Left:** Lively cascades on the Swale at Richmond, the 100-foot (30m) keep of whose eleventh-century castle can be glimpsed on the skyline. The Swale, 73 miles (118km) long, is rated England's fastest-flowing river.

**Opposite:** Haylands Bridge, an elegant arched structure between Hawes and Sedbusk in Wensleydale, carries Brunt Acres Road across the Ure, close to its confluence with Widdale Beck.

# Mystic Rivers

**Far left:** Autumn leaves pepper the rocks at the Strid, where the Wharfe, in a delightfully wooded part of its course, rushes angrily through a natural bottleneck on the Bolton Abbey estate.

**Top left:** Dramatic lighting in the heart of Littondale, with the Skirfare in good form. The Skirfare flows into the Wharfe just north of Kilnsey.

**Bottom left:** A tranquil scene, so typical of sleepy Raydale, along the banks of the Bain. This river, which flows out of Semer Water, is just two and a half miles (4km) long and is said to be the shortest in England.

**Right:** The Wharfe, not far from its source, races over its rocky bed in Langstrothdale. The road through this valley parallels the river and provides excellent views of it.

# Shore Leave

Reflected glory at Semer Water, the shallow natural lake which graces beautiful Raydale and is a haven for plant, bird and wild life. Legend says a city once stood here. A weary old traveller, unhappy with his reception as he sought food and shelter, put a curse on the city, which, as he predicted, was inundated and vanished without trace.

# Plenty in Reserve

**Left:** Spectacular lighting at Embsay Reservoir, with Embsay Crag's distinctive outline completing a dramatic scene. The reservoir, opened in 1910, was constructed to meet rising demand in the Skipton area.

**Top:** Late afternoon sun illuminates the ornate dam at Angram Reservoir, one of three in Nidderdale. The central castellated tower is used for drawing off water. Angram, amid bleak scenery close to the valley head, was completed in 1919 to supply the Bradford area.

**Bottom:** Autumn shades are reflected in the surface of Fewston Reservoir, located between Otley and Pateley Bridge in the picturesque Washburn Valley.

# Special Branch

**Opposite:** For colour and aroma, springtime in a wood is hard to beat. This beautiful study in light and shade was captured amid the trees of Skipton Woods.

**Below:** The extensive Bolton Abbey Estate, with its network of footpaths close to the banks of the Wharfe, offers some of the finest woodland walking in the Dales, as this charming autumnal view illustrates.

**Far left:** Southerscales is the vantage point for this dramatic perspective of Ingleborough, which reaches a height of 2,372 feet (723m). This distinctively profiled peak is dubbed the Blue Hill, a nickname seemingly inappropriate on the rare occasions that Ingleborough is as well lit as this.

**Middle:** The impressive snow-tipped nose of Ribblesdale's Crouching Lion, as Penyghent is affectionately nicknamed. With its summit at 2,277 feet (694m), the mountain is the lowest of the Three Peaks, but a firm favourite among visitors to this spectacular valley.

**Left:** The ominous bulk of Whernside, at 2,415 feet (736m) the highest of the Three Peaks, viewed across the limestone splendour of Twisleton Scar, high above Chapel-le-Dale. The boulder in the foreground is a glacial erratic.

# Limestone Wonders

**Right:** Gordale Beck in full flow, with the slightly menacing 'jaws' of Gordale Scar beyond. This awesome limestone chasm was scooped out by repeated glacial action.

**Middle:** Part of Malham Cove, a curving limestone crag 260 feet (80m) high and 985 feet (300m) long, finds itself drenched in sunshine.

**Inset:** A detailed perspective of a section of limestone pavement at Ribblehead, a district noted for such a feature. The eroded gaps are known as grikes and the hardier 'teeth' are called clints.

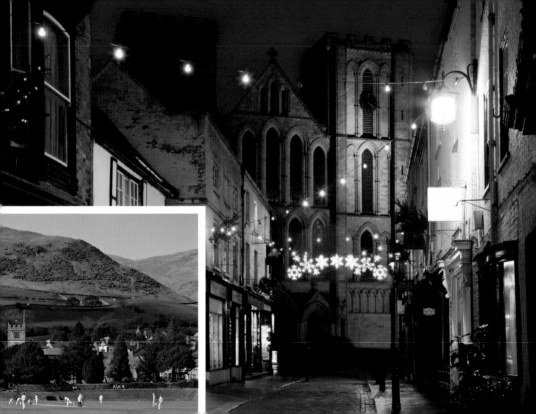

# Going to Town

**Far left:** The historic city of Ripon is dominated by the magnificent thirteenth-century cathedral church of St Peter and St Wilfrid, the west front of which looks particularly impressive in this atmospheric view of Kirkgate.

**Inset:** There cannot be many prettier cricket grounds in the North than the main square at Sedbergh School, seen here with the town and the lower slopes of the eastern Howgills combining to form a glorious backdrop.

**Left:** Winter has a firm hold on Pateley Bridge, the bustling capital of upper Nidderdale, in this snowy picture looking down High Street towards the bridge over the River Nidd.

# Community Service

**Top left:** The sloping green at Reeth, a lively community always busy with visitors, and formerly a hub of the leadmining industry. It is positioned on the lower slopes of Calver Hill at the junction of Swaledale and Arkengarthdale.

**Bottom left:** Daffodils ignite Malham in spring, with the pretty banks of Malham Beck guaranteeing a colourful display of blooms.

**Right:** The bridge over Dowber Gill Beck in the heart of Kettlewell, whose whitewashed pubs are a welcome sight for thirsty visitors.

**Overleaf left:** Grassington's cobbled square, picturesque by day, acquires an extra magic once night has fallen. It is the stage for a Dickensian Festival, held annually in early December.

**Overleaf right:** Askrigg, a Wensleydale jewel, nestles beneath the table-top summit of Addlebrough, which rises to 1,564 feet (477m). Years ago, this delightful village was more important than neighbouring Hawes.

# Community Service

**Left:** Haphazardly arranged cottages are a key element in the appeal of many Dales villages, a characteristic seen to good effect at Hawes.

**Middle:** West Burton, tucked away at the entrance to lonely Waldendale, boasts one of the largest village greens in England and an array of attractive dwellings.

**Below:** The landmark tower of the Parish Church of St Mary the Virgin dominates Muker, a charming village on the banks of Straw Beck in upper Swaledale.

# Gimme Shelter

**Right:** Late eighteenth- and early nineteenth-century barns – or 'laithes' in Yorkshire dialect – are an endearing feature of Swaledale. A pristine example of these appealing structures dominates this wintry view of the valley between Keld and Thwaite.

**Inset top:** An almost monochromatic Swaledale scene in which a barn and drystone walls provide a sharp contrast to deep, crisp and even snow.

**Inset bottom:** Wensleydale is one of several Dales valleys whose appearance is enhanced by traditional barns, as these weathered neighbours illustrate.

**Above:** The remnants of lead mining along Old Gang Beck, between Swaledale and Arkengarthdale, are the most extensive in the Dales. The ruinous smelt mill, the main part of which was built about 1828, is a Scheduled Ancient Monument.

**Above right:** The atmospheric int Hoffman kiln at the former Craver in Langcliffe. This remarkable str Scheduled Ancient Monument, w 1873. Firing ceased here shortly outbreak of war in 1939.

# Palaces of Industry

Right: The poignant ruin of Swinner Gill smelt mill, built for Lord Pomfret in 1804, occupies a grand perch above a small waterfall. An entrance to a lead mining level can be seen to the left of the stream in this steep-sided valley, a tributary of Swaledale.

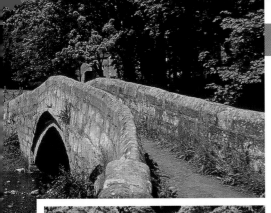

# Mind the Gap

**Left:** South Dean Beck is crossed, between Haworth and Top Withins, by the delightful Brontë Bridge, an attractive clapper design whose name celebrates the district's well-known literary associations.

**Middle:** There are many crossings of Linton Beck in and around the eponymous village in Wharfedale, but none prettier than this ancient packhorse bridge next to the green.

**Inset:** A walker's-eye view of a lovely footbridge over Whitfield Beck, upstream of bonny Askrigg in Wensleydale.

**Left:** The eleven arches of Ingleton Viaduct, 80 feet (24m) off the ground, bestride the village. It is on a route intended originally to provide a fast link to Scotland. But the line never developed beyond a quiet rural branch and closed to all traffic in 1967.

**Right:** Ribblehead Viaduct, whose twenty-four arches are the most eyecatching feature on the Settle-Carlisle Railway. It took an army of navvies, living in shanty towns nearby, four years to build the 104-foot (32m) high structure, whose impressive dimensions are dwarfed by Whernside.

# Arch Rivals

# Man the Ramparts

**Left:** The impressive sandstone towers of Bolton Castle, which have dominated mid-Wensleydale since 1399. Mary, Queen of Scots was a prisoner here between 1568 and 1569.

**Top right:** Richmond Castle's great keep stands 100 feet (30m) high on a rocky promontory above the fast-flowing waters of the Swale.

**Bottom right:** The builders of Skipton Castle certainly knew how to make an entrance. The medieval structure's imposing twin-towered gatehouse is unmissable from High Street.

**Below:** Dazzling spring flowers are a feature of Knaresborough Castle's grounds, which overlook the Nidd Gorge and provide one of Yorkshire's most cherished views.

# Man the Ramparts

**Left:** Through the arched window: the ruins of twelfth-century Middleham Castle, childhood home of Richard III.

**Right:** This ornamental weir drains the lake at Ripley Castle, home to the Ingilby family for twenty-six generations.

# The Power of Faith

**Left:** The view towards the altar at Hubberholme's riverside church, which boasts one of only two rood lofts in Yorkshire. Fashioned from oak, the rood loft is 500 years old. Kilburn craftsman Robert 'Mouseman' Thompson carved the pews, while Bradford-born author and dramatist J B Priestley is buried nearby.

**Top:** St Oswald's, on the tree-fringed banks of the Skirfare in the Littondale village of Arncliffe, boasts one of the prettiest settings of any church in Yorkshire.

**Middle:** Vibrant stained-glass depicting a soldier in the parish church of St Andrew, Sedbergh.

**Bottom:** Few would be surprised to learn that lovely Linton lies at the end of a rainbow. The Wharfedale village's distinctively squat church, dedicated to St Michael and All Angels, is positioned on a bend in the river and dates from the twelfth century.

# The Abbey Habit

**Top left:** Floodlighting picks out the intricate carving in the crypt at Fountains Abbey.

**Bottom left:** Twelfth-century Augustinian canons could scarcely have chosen a more picturesque setting for Bolton Priory, and its starkly romantic ruins are particularly dramatic when viewed from the opposite bank of the adjacent River Wharfe.

**Right:** Fountains Abbey, constructed on the banks of the River Skell by Cistercian monks in the twelfth and thirteenth centuries, is Yorkshire's first World Heritage Site. Abandoned in 1539, the rambling structure's extensive remains are hugely impressive.

# Halls of Fame

**Left:** Harewood House, a mid-eighteenth century mansion on the northern outskirts of Leeds. The house is seen across landscaped grounds laid out by Lancelot 'Capability' Brown.

**Top:** A charming scene in the gardens at Parcevall Hall, a Dales gem hidden away in the valley of Skyreholme Beck. The hillside gardens were the brainchild of plantsman Sir William Milner, who began his pet project in 1927.

**Bottom:** Seventeenth-century elegance at Newby Hall, near Ripon. Renowned architect Sir Christopher Wren designed the house, whose extensive grounds contain the longest double herbaceous borders in England.

# Putting on a Show

**Top right:** Nothing evokes that 'Yorkshire' feeling like the sound of brass. A band belts out one of its favourite numbers to entertain the crowds at Muker Show, a popular event staged on the first Wednesday in September.

**Bottom right:** Runners dig deep during a typically gruelling fell race, one of many traditional events staged each June at Buckden Gala.

**Far right:** Masham Sheep Fair, held annually in the autumn, takes over the town's rambling market square, and celebrates an era when regular fairs were staged.

# The Great Outdoors

**Far left:** A climber ponders his next move as he scales the sheer limestone face of Malham Cove, one of the most remarkable natural features in the Dales.

**Left:** Walkers stroll across the apron of grass leading towards Cautley Crag and Spout in the eastern Howgills. With a steep ascent in prospect, the hard yards are very much ahead.

**Inset:** Cyclists head east through Castle Bolton to a spectacular backdrop of the sleepy village's fourteenth-century fortress.

# Colours of Nature

**Right:** Upper Swaledale's wildflower meadows are seen at their best in spring when they are transformed by a brilliant carpet of buttercups.

**Top left:** Frost has left its artistic mark on these fallen leaves at Harlow Carr Gardens on the western edge of Harrogate. The gardens, one of four in Britain run by the Royal Horticultural Society, celebrated its sixtieth anniversary in 2010.

**Bottom left:** Valley Gardens, in Low Harrogate, are a delight throughout the year. The 17-acre (7ha) site is home to many beautiful species, including this superb Cornell dahlia.

# Golden Goodbye

**Left:** With the sun about to dip below the western horizon, Malham Tarn's glassy surface reflects like a mirror. At 1,237 feet (377m), it is the highest lake in England.

**Middle:** Farewell to a winter's day on the Chevin, high above the Wharfedale market town of Otley.

**Below:** Ingleborough's outline, silhouetted against the setting sun, is unmistakeable in this snowy upland panorama.

# Index

# Photographic Acknowledgements

Andy Aughey, p13; Howard Beck, back cover middle, pp7, 42 right; Lee Beel (www.lee-beel-photography.co.uk), p60 top; Dorothy Burrows, pp41 left, 49; Neil Burton (www.neilburton.smugmug.com), pp12 right, 14 left, 18 top left, 19, 38 bottom, 48; Chris Caeser (www.chrisceaser.com), pp16, 16, 24; Chris Dyson (www.chrisdysonphotography.com ), p47 bottom right, 63; Kevin Eaves, p58 right; Derek Forss (www.derekforss.com), pp30 inset, 51 middle; Steve Gosling (www.stevegoslingphotography. co.uk), p60 bottom; Fran Halsall (www.fran-halsall.co.uk), pp27, 38 top; Granville Harris (www.granvilleharrisphotography.co.uk), pp22, 26 left; Andrew Hopkins, back cover bottom left & bottom right, pp4, 9, 12 left, 25, 30, 32 bottom, 33, 34, 37, 52 top, 56 bottom, 58 left; Wayne Hutchinson, p8 ( www.farm-images.co.uk); Mike Kipling (www.mikekiplingstockphotos. co.uk), pp35, 36 left & right, 39, 44, 52 bottom, 53, 54, 55 bottom, 56 top, 59 bottom, 61; Andy Latham (www.andylatham.co.uk), pp5, 6 top left, 11 bottom right & top left, 18 bottom left, 29 left; Jeanie Lazenby, p45; Andrew Linscott (www.andrewlinscott.co.uk), p31; Andrew Miles, p11 bottom right; Simon Miles ( www.simonmilesphotography.co.uk), p62 right; John Morrison, p50, 51 bottom, 62 left; John Potter (www.jpotter-landscape-photographer.com), front cover, back cover top, pp6 right, 10, 29 right, 32 top, 46, 51 top, 55 top, 57; Paul Ridsdale, p47 bottom left; Anita Skinner, p47 top right; Mark Sunderland (www.marksunderland.com), pp5 right, 14 right, 18 left 23 top & bottom, 26 right, 28 bottom, 42 left; David Taylor (www.davidtaylorphotography.co.uk), p43 right; Keith Wood (www.keithwoodphotography.co.uk), pp17, 20-21, 40, 41 right.